Snakes Awake

JARROD PAINE SHANNON BOLAND

FORD ST

I love exploring the bush,
especially in summer.

Mum and I go to the river
to see what we can find.

We always wear boots and
long pants so we don't get
scratched or stung or bitten.

Lots of things live in the bush.

Mum always says,
'Be prepared!'

She carries our backpack
with a phone, a first-aid kit,
a water bottle . . .

and yummy snacks.

WALKING TRACK
BATTY
Round Plain
Paradise
MOUNT NELSE NORTH
MOUNT NELSE
Johnston Hut
ALPINE WALKING TRACK
Edmonson Hut
Kelly Hut
Fitzgerald Hut
KELLY
Creek
BIG
Walking
Track
RIVER
Dead
Horse
Wild
HEATHY
Aqueduct
BASALT
SPUR
BASALT HILL
VALLEY STORAGE
Wallace Gap
MAGNETIC NORTH
Shannonvale
SHANNONVALE
BOGONG
Cemetery
Wills
Bog
Al

We walk on wide-open tracks that we know.
Mum always goes first.
I look for animal tracks and poo with my special nature goggles.

Sometimes we see skinks lying in the sun.
If I'm quick I can catch them.

I hold them gently so they're not hurt.

Last week we saw a snake!
It was so cool.

Mum saw it first.
She lifted me up so I could see too.
It was lying across the track
having a snooze in the sun.

It was a beautiful red-bellied black snake – my favourite kind. How lucky was that!

The snake must have felt our footsteps because it woke up and slowly slithered away.

Last summer we gave a snake a fright.
It lifted its head up in an S shape
and tried to act tough.

We quietly backed away. We watched the scaredy snake slither off towards the river. It was exciting!

I wonder what it would be like to sleep with your eyes open like a snake?

Sometimes I try to slither along on my tummy.

It's hard!

I really like snakes.

I always look out for them, and if I see one,
I watch it from a safe distance.

Sometimes I have to remind Mum to check before she steps over a log.

Sometimes she has to remind me to watch where I put my hand on the bank beside the track.

Once our neighbours had to
phone the snake catcher.

There were lots of good hiding places
in their backyard.

She came and rescued
the snake with special tools
so it wouldn't be hurt,

then she let it go
in the bush.

I love our bushwalks.

If I'm lucky,
I get to see snakes.
And they're amazing.

Safety facts

To explore the Australian bush safely, especially in summer:

Wear long pants and sturdy footwear.

Carry water, snacks, a phone, first-aid kit with a snake-bite compression bandage, and a map if you're going somewhere new.

Have an adult walk at the front of the group to spot and manage dangers.

Look over logs before stepping over them and watch where you put your hands on the bank next to the track.

Watch where you sit down, too!

If you see wildlife, keep a safe distance away – a car length or more is best.

If the animal is showing signs of distress or fear, move away carefully. Otherwise, enjoy watching it.

First aid for snake bite

If someone is bitten by a snake, or thinks they have been bitten:

1. First make sure everyone is safe.

2. Phone 000 for an ambulance.

3. Calm the person and help them lie down and keep very still. (Venom moves through your lymphatic system only when you move muscles.)

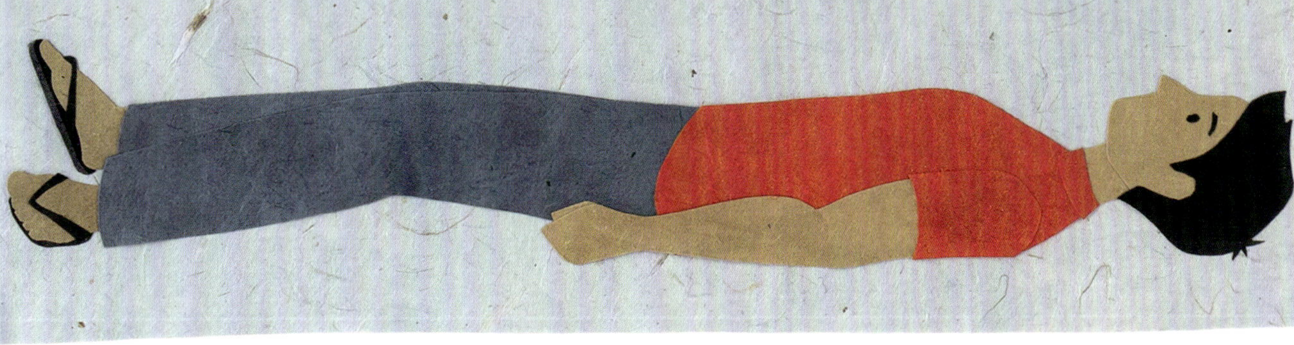

4. Apply a compression bandage to the wound then bandage firmly and evenly down to just above the fingers or toes then up the limb as far as it will reach. If you don't have a bandage, you can make do with any stretchy fabric, such as a T-shirt.

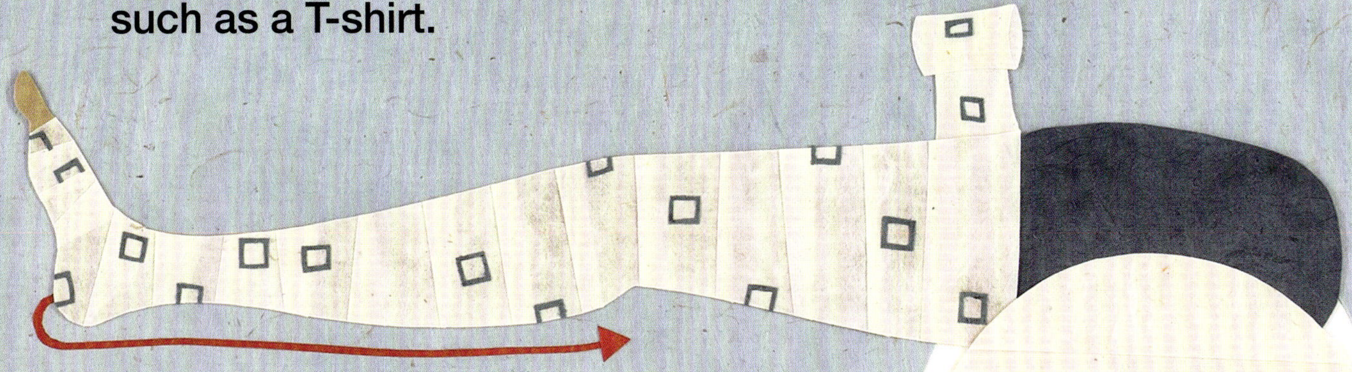

5 Mark the bite on the bandage with a pen if you have one.

6. Splint the limb so it can't move.

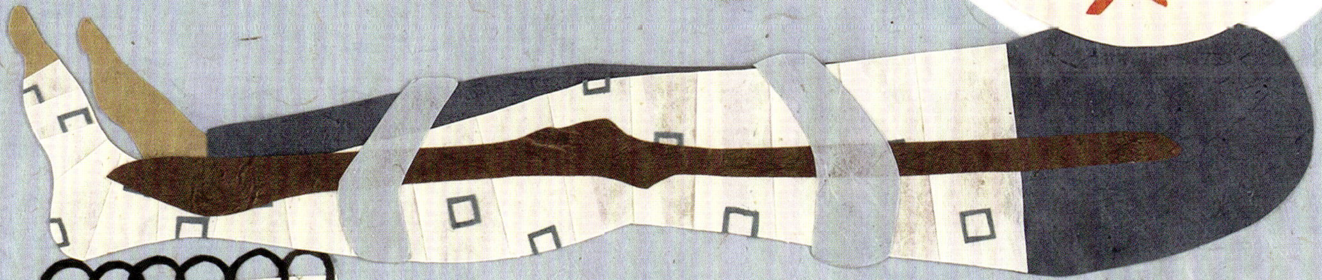

7. Write down when the snake bite happened and when the bandage was applied.

For Jemima and Griffin, who sparked my passion for communicating the wonders of nature – JP

For Liam – SB

First published by Ford Street Publishing, Melbourne, Victoria, Australia

2 4 6 8 10 9 7 5 3 1

ISBN: 9781925804935 (hardcover)
ISBN: 9781925804928 (paperback)

Ford Street website: www.fordstreetpublishing.com
First published 2022

NATIONAL LIBRARY OF AUSTRALIA
A catalogue record for this book is available from the National Library of Australia

Design and layout: Cathy Larsen Design
Editorial: Nan McNab
Printed in China by Tingleman Pty Ltd

Map on p. 7 courtesy Department of Environment, Land, Water and Planning (DELWP)

Media used: layered paper accented with coloured pencil and gouache